THE LITTLE BOOK OF
TRAVIS KELCE

First published in 2024 by OH
An Imprint of HEADLINE PUBLISHING GROUP

2 4 6 8 10 9 7 5 3 1

Disclaimer:

Cataloguing in Publication Data is available from the British Library

ISBN 978-1-03542-102-2

Compiled and written by: David Clayton
Editorial: Saneaah Muhammad
Designed and typeset in Avenir by: Andy Jones
Project manager: Russell Porter
Production: Arlene Lestrade
Printed and bound in China

HEADLINE PUBLISHING GROUP
An Hachette UK Company
Carmelite House, 50 Victoria Embankment, London EC4Y 0DZ

www.headline.co.uk   www.hachette.co.uk

THE LITTLE BOOK OF
TRAVIS KELCE

IN HIS OWN WORDS

CONTENTS

INTRODUCTION – 6

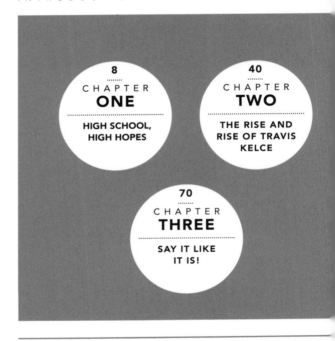

8

CHAPTER
ONE

HIGH SCHOOL,
HIGH HOPES

40

CHAPTER
TWO

THE RISE AND
RISE OF TRAVIS
KELCE

70

CHAPTER
THREE

SAY IT LIKE
IT IS!

90

CHAPTER
FOUR

FAMILY,
FRIENDS, AND
HEROES

120

CHAPTER
FIVE

THE HISTORY
BOY

158

CHAPTER
SIX

TALK OF THE
TOWN

INTRODUCTION

Those with even a passing knowledge of American football were well acquainted with Travis Kelce long before a certain popstar entered the scene. Considered one of the best tight ends in history, the Kansas City Chiefs player is a three-time Super Bowl champion and holder of multiple NFL records.

His fame reached new heights, though, when rumours started swirling about a relationship between him and global megastar Taylor Swift—and their relationship has since gone from strength to strength.

Now a household name around the world, Travis has also featured in an Amazon Prime documentary, has appeared on a dating game show dedicated to him, and has a smash-hit podcast—*New Heights*—with his brother, Jason, that regularly tops the Apple and Spotify charts.

Beyond that, though, Travis is also funny, outspoken, and charming, and it's not hard to see why Taylor fell for him. A philanthropist, role model for millions, and always the first to poke fun at himself, Travis Kelce is a sports and media phenomenon—and, right now, everything seems to be going his way.

The Little Book of Travis Kelce encapsulates every aspect of Travis's life, from his podcast to his documentary, his touchdowns to his Super Bowl rings, and his relationship with one of the biggest popstars ever.

So grab your 87 jersey, and get ready to kick off.

Chapter 1

High School, High Hopes

Born to be an NFL superstar, Travis's humble beginnings playing sports with his family shaped him into the man he is today.

The start of the journey, the dreams of being an NFL superstar, and the bumps along the way... it's all right here.

High School, High Hopes

I grew up in Cleveland Heights. It wasn't just the house that made me, Cleveland Heights, the home, the community, it was very multicultural, different ethnicities to different social classes. I just have so much love for the people in that city. It's given me so many different ways to appreciate life. And one of them is definitely the sports world.

On the origin of his love for sport, The Players' Tribune, December 2, 2020.

The Facts #1

Travis Michael Kelce was born in Cleveland Heights, Ohio, on October 5, 1989. He attended Cleveland Heights High School, where he played football, basketball, and baseball, though it was as a quarterback in football that he initially excelled.

My dad just kind of got lazy and didn't really wanna keep correcting everybody that was calling him Kell-see, so he just went along with Kell-see.

Revealing the correct pronunciation of his surname—"Kellss" not "Kell-cee"! *Bussin' With The Boys* podcast, July 2021.

"

I got kicked out of pre-school because during playtime we were playing checkers, and I was winning because I don't f***ing lose at checkers and if you win you stay on.

"

Explaining the story behind when he threw a chair at his teacher and his competitive nature, pagesix.com, September 2022.

High School, High Hopes

I was always a kid that never wanted to be in my room. If my dad told me, 'Time out and you gotta go to your room', that was the worst thing ever. Because I was always wanting to be outside.

On playing outside during his childhood, The Players' Tribune, December 2, 2020.

66

I played every game you can imagine. Football, soccer—my dad got us into handball 'cause we kept breaking windows.

99

On the sports he played as a child, The Players' Tribune, December 2, 2020.

High School, High Hopes

We had almost like our own little sports complex at the house. The driveway was like the pitching mound. We used to play one-on-one street hockey right there. My dad wanted to make sure we were ready to have some fun, so he was always out grabbing sports equipment. It didn't matter how old the equipment was, as long as we had some equipment to play with, we were going to figure it out.

On his family home being the first sports arena he played in, The Players' Tribune, December 2, 2020.

"

He pushed us to want to win the game and he pushed us to want to get better. But at the same time, he's laughing through it all and making sure that we're having as much fun as he is.

"

On his dad's support from a young age,
The Players' Tribune, December 2, 2020.

High School, High Hopes

Sports for me was where I built my confidence. You probably won't believe me, but I was a shy kid growing up until I got onto the sports field, or the court or the ice rink. Then I kind of let my personality show. I was having fun. I was having success. And that's just kind of propelled me to have confidence in life.

Reflecting on the feeling sports gave him as a kid, Super Bowl LVIII Press Conference, February 2024.

66

I'm very fortunate that I had a household that allowed me to live so carefree and so happy. It all roots from those days, me in the backyard, and finding a love for the game and the love for life.

99

On growing up in a supportive household, The Players' Tribune, December 2, 2020.

Throwing the ball around with Pops, that was everything as a kid. If I could get out and do that every single day, I was as happy as could be. Like the day was the best day ever.

On the happiness he felt playing sports as a child, The Players' Tribune, December 2, 2020.

66

Those little moments, that just running around, seeing the ball come my way and screwing up one time, my dad telling me what I did wrong or how to do something better, those moments are what fuels the love that I still have for the game.

99

On his memories of learning how to play sports games as a child, The Players' Tribune, December 2, 2020.

The Facts #2

Travis accepted a scholarship at the University of Cincinnati, turning down offers from Akron, East Michigan, and Miami. After progressing well in college football, he was suspended for the 2010 season aged 18 for testing positive for marijuana use, but after returning focused and determined, he was voted Tight End of the Year at the 2013 College Football Awards.

66

I got kicked off the team, scholarship was revoked, and I got to live with the embarrassment of it, and I got to live with trying to get back into the university, so I could try and work my way back onto the team.

99

Revealing how his failed drugs test could have ruined his hopes of becoming a professional footballer, *Kelce* (2023).

I was finally playing college football and having a blast. I was partying my ass off.

On his wild time in college, *Kelce* (2023).

"

My mom visited one time when Travis was suspended. She smells something and walks downstairs in the basement and it's Trav— smoking a joint. She goes: 'Travis, aren't you suspended for this?!?'

"

College housemate Zach Collaros recalls his mother's visit to their digs in Cincinnati, *Daily Mail*, February 2024.

I know I didn't make everybody really that proud. It was the first time that I had ever really hit adversity.

On the shame and disappointment he felt after his failed drugs test, *Kelce* (2023).

66

I'm just sitting there, dead in the water. I just wanted to get out of there. I was so embarrassed, I didn't want to look at anybody.

99

On failing the NCAA drug test and being banned for 12 months, *Vanity Fair*, June 28, 2023.

High School, High Hopes

I told him it's a great learning opportunity. Live with it. Grow from it. Learn from it. It is what it is, and you just have to deal with it now. All the while, I'm biting my tongue about how stupid it is that they're going to suspend a college kid for smoking pot. Give me a f***ing break.

Ed Kelce

Travis's father telling his son what he needs to hear, even if he doesn't agree with the punishment, *Vanity Fair*, June 28, 2023.

"
I thought football was over
for me.

"

On his despair after being suspended from college
football for the entire 2010 season at the University
of Cincinnati having failed a drug test for marijuana,
Kansas City Star, March 6, 2023.

High School, High Hopes

I made sure to tell them don't hold back, tell all the good stories. And sure enough they mentioned all the really good ones, like Zach's mom walking in on me firing up in the garage before one of the games. Absolutely hilarious. That's how I was living back then. **"**

Revealing that he actively encourages his friends to speak openly about their time together in interviews, *Daily Mail*, February 2024.

"

It was a filthy, but so much f****ng fun, house, man. Endless memories.

"

On his wild college days under the "watchful" eye of brother Jason, *Daily Mail*, February 2024.

High School, High Hopes

"

Jason and I have actually been playing football together since we were little kids, and he was always better than me—at everything. In high school, he was an honor student and I got kicked off the team because I failed French. And then, when we were in college, I actually got kicked off the team because I tested positive for marijuana.

"

Paying tribute to his big brother, *Saturday Night Live,* February 2023.

"

I really started hitting the weights. It became clear that I needed to get much stronger if I was going to do this. Even when I was getting beat every day, I would stay positive by telling myself stuff like, 'Listen, I'm every bit as good as this guy across from me.' The thing is, you are every bit of what you think of yourself. If you think you can improve, it'll happen.

"

On the learning process and working out, The Players' Tribune, October 7, 2016.

High School, High Hopes

"

As a kid, I always dreamed of being an NFL quarterback. I remember being 10 years old and saying, 'Mom… I'm gonna throw a football in the NFL, and it's going to be a touchdown, and everybody's gonna love it.'

"

On his dream of playing in the NFL, albeit he became a tight end rather than a quarterback, The Players' Tribune, May 1, 2018.

The Facts #3

Kelce was drafted by Kansas City Chiefs for the 2013 NFL draft when he was 63rd overall pick. Chiefs' head coach Andy Reid signed Travis on the basis that he had coached his brother Jason when he'd been in charge of Philadelphia Eagles—Jason had convinced Reid to give Travis a chance. Travis signed a four-year deal worth $3.13m plus an extra $700,000 signing-on fee.

High School, High Hopes

I look forward to playing them just because they're the Cincinnati Bengals. I went to the University of Cincinnati, and they picked a tight end over me in the draft. You can't tell me that they didn't do that. I was sitting right back there in their backyard.

On the Cincinnati Bengals, *Daily Mail*, December 2023.

66

They definitely completely just said, 'F*** you, Travis.'

99

Revealing that the Cincinnati Bengals' decision to overlook him in the 2013 draft still fires him up whenever the two teams face each other, *Daily Mail*, December 2023.

Perfection is when the finality of a process meets the expectations you have dreamed of… And I've never had a dream come true…

On perfection and dreams, Twitter, October 2012.

"

He caught me at a moment in my life where I was down in the dumps. I didn't really think much of myself. When I got hit with what I was going through, I found out how many people were in my corner.

"

On Butch Jones, his coach at the University of Cincinnati, *Vanity Fair*, June 28, 2023.

Chapter 2

The Rise and Rise of Travis Kelce

Despite his rocky start in the world of American football, Travis was given a second chance.

The opportunity to show what he was really capable of began the day he joined Kansas City Chiefs...

The Rise and Rise of Travis Kelce

"

He immediately takes it right back to the floor and says, 'Listen, man, this is serious, no goofing around,' and a whole lot of words that I would rather not repeat. He basically said, 'Do not screw this up.'

"

Recalling his phone call with Kansas City Chiefs head coach Andy Reid after being offered a second chance to build a career, *Club Shay Shay* podcast, 2021.

"

[Reid's] helped me a lot with that, channeling my emotion. I owe my entire career to that guy and being able to control how emotional I get.

"

On how head coach Andy Reid helped him to control his emotions on the field, *ESPN*, February 12, 2024.

It's not that I did something, it's more that some guys see it, you just have to convince them that they have talent, and they can have a better future going down this path than the other path.

Jason Avant

The retired NFL wide receiver guiding Travis down the right path, *Daily Mail*, January 2024.

"

Travis Kelce is a perfectionist. I remember when coach Andy Reid took me there to help Kelce develop into a professional because he had a lot of immaturities coming out of college. He had a lot of issues, and it was my job to help.

"

Jason Avant

Reflecting on his mentoring of Travis, *Daily Mail*, January 2024.

The Rise and Rise of Travis Kelce

He could have killed me, but he was every bit of a mentor in those moments, man. Along the way there was some tough brother shit that I just had to hear, and I knew my brother had gone to the coaches and said, 'You know, if you give him a second chance, he won't screw up.' It kind of put his word on the line… Without that guy, I don't know where [or] what I would be doing.

On his brother's strong faith in him, *Kelce* (2023).

66

I'm so fortunate to get tossed in this organization at this time. I'm just reaping the benefits.

99

Relishing in his "second chance" after being picked up by Kansas City Chiefs, *Vanity Fair*, June 28, 2023.

No matter what your experience level or how great you are, you're going to take a shot at some point.

On taking risks as a tight end, The Players' Tribune, October 7, 2016.

66

Do you stay down or do you get back up and pop 'em in the mouth on the next play? That's what defines you as a player. More than anything else, that's what makes a great tight end.

99

On what makes a great tight end, The Players' Tribune, October 7, 2016.

66

Never get comfortable.
Constantly challenge yourself to
push your limits!

99

On challenging his comfort zone, X, March 24, 2014.

"

I just always felt comfortable with the camera on me and the lights on me. Sure enough, I love a good challenge. I get excited for a challenge.

"

On welcoming challenges and feeling comfortable in the spotlight, *BANG Showbiz*, April 2024.

At the end of the day, I feel like if you're not having fun with what you do, there's really not much of a point to be doing it.

On doing what you love, ESPN, January 12, 2017.

66

Once you have success, you have
to maintain success.

99

*On the journey of success, Sports Illustrated,
January 31, 2018.*

My actions on the field are very—I don't want to say emotional, but emotion does get the best of me out there. If I do something wrong, I'm livid. I take it that seriously.

On emotion affecting action, *GQ*, September 7, 2017.

"
I like to think of it as I have passion more than I have emotion. Emotion comes and goes. It goes up and down like a rollercoaster. Passion sits in the heart; it's within you.
"

On his passion and emotion, Arrowhead Pride, April 17, 2020.

The Rise and Rise of Travis Kelce

I started playing this game in the backyard, I started playing this game in middle school and going to go practice without any fans, without any sounds.

On his early days playing basketball, Arrowhead Pride, April 17, 2020.

66

All I been doing is playing outside, playing sports my entire life.

99

On sports being his dream career from a young age, ESPN, January 12, 2017.

The Rise and Rise of Travis Kelce

I had played quarterback my entire life up until that point. I always thought that if all of those other schools were right and I was meant to be a tight end, it wouldn't be too difficult to make the switch. I mean, I was tall and fast, with decent hands. How hard could it be? It's really damn hard.

On making the switch from quarterback to tight end, The Players' Tribune, October 7, 2016.

"

Being able to get a big body to change direction, I think that's huge. I don't think a lot of tight ends incorporate that enough. I got a lot of that from playing hockey when I was younger, being able to play on the inside and outside of skates, as well as on the basketball court, being able to put my foot into the ground and crossover.

"

On being able to train his body to be an exceptional tight end.

I get most of my athleticism from my mom. I know my dad cringes every single time I say that, but my competitive nature was always fueled by my dad.

On his dad being the inspiration behind his love of sport.

66

As a blocker, that gets you excited, man. You've got somebody who can take it to the house at any point in the game, and you want to make sure that you get your guy that much more.

99

On the exciting positions that could make or break a football game.

There's nothing you can really say to a loved one in [a] situation like that. You joke around all the time and say that you want to be your brother on the biggest stage ever. But it's a weird feeling. It's a weird feeling, and that team has had great leadership and great coaches; obviously, it came down to the end. And we got all the respect in the world for those Eagles, man, but, there's nothing really I could say to him other than I love him. And that he played a hell of a year, a hell of a season.

99

Reflecting on an emotional Super Bowl against brother Jason, *USA Today*, February 2023.

It's definitely cool that guys can come together, in all this chaos and madness, and change their lives in a positive way.

On the spirituality of his teammates and their openness in the locker room, starbeliefs.com, 2024.

66

Gotta be a better teammate gotta be a better leader... plain and simple.

99

Looking to the season ahead, and aspiring to be an example on the pitch, X, July 2023.

I feel like this was the happiest year of my life, man.

Reflecting on an unbelievable 12 months—unaware that the next 12 would be even better! Chiefswire, February 2023.

"

I think this is absolutely stupid,
I don't think this is making the game
safe; I think it's making it more
boring and taking a lot of excitement
out of the game's opening play.
This is whack.

"

Expressing his views on the NFL's decision
to adopt a new kick-off rule, allowing kick returners
to call a fair catch and subsequently start the
offensive drive from the 25-yard line, Brobible,
May 2023.

The Rise and Rise of Travis Kelce

I enjoy making people laugh.
If I can put a smile on someone's
face if I do a dance in the end
zone, why not?

99

On bringing positivity to football games.

66
You can kind of just move me
around and put me anywhere—
whatever the coaches and the guys
on this team need me to do.
99

On being able to play any position in a
football game.

Chapter 3

Say It Like It Is!

Straight-talking, funny, and
inspirational—Travis Kelce not only
talks a good game, but he plays one,
too… and that includes helping
those less fortunate.

Say It Like It Is!

66

Burrowhead my ass, it's Mahomes' house!

99

Responding to Cincinnati Mayor Aftab Pureval's trash talk ahead of AFC 2023 championship game—a fired-up Chiefs won this encounter 23-20. Biography.com, 2023.

"

Know your role, and shut your mouth, you jabroni.

"

Further chastising Cincinnati Mayor Pureval with a famous catchphrase by Dwayne "The Rock" Johnson. Pureval later admitted he "deserved that". Biography.com, 2023.

My boy said what he said.
I appreciate the venomous 'shut yo'
over formal 'shut your.'

Dwayne "The Rock" Johnson
Responding to Travis's jabroni tribute, X, 2023.

66

I feel like when you're on the
platform where you can influence
a lot of people, you should take
advantage of that and do it in the
proper way.

99

On using his fame and fortune for good,
NFL Players Association, April 12, 2015.

The Facts #4

In 2015, Travis started his charitable foundation Eighty-Seven & Running to help young people who didn't have the same opportunities he did to become productive citizens by mentoring and motivating them to explore and develop their abilities while learning critical life skills. The foundation creates enrichment opportunities for youth and their communities through fundraising, athletic programs, mentoring, and outreach initiatives.

"

Joining forces with my friends over at Kodiak to fuel the Operation Breakthrough families is a total privilege. Alongside Kodiak, a brand I love, we will be making a meaningful difference in the day-to-day life of hundreds of Kansas City kids, and I couldn't be more excited to make this happen.

"

Kelce teamed up with breakfast cereal brand Kodiak in an initiative to provide 25,000 free meals, 2022.

Say It Like It Is!

I am heartbroken over the tragedy that took place today. My heart is with all who came out to celebrate with us and have been affected. KC, you mean the world to me.

Responding to the Kansas Super Bowl parade shootings, X, February 2024.

"

Travis Kelce has been giving back big to his hometown schools, and we are grateful. Because of his generosity, more than 2,300 children have had access to remote learning supports, after school enrichment, tutoring programs, and inspirational speakers. He's setting an amazing example for our kids and for our alumni.

"

Julianna Johnston Senturia

The Executive Director of the Heights Schools Foundation praising Travis's philanthropy.

Just to see the smiles on their faces when they're grabbing gifts for their mothers and fathers, that makes you feel good.

Kelce and JCPenney donated a $100 gift card to each of the 25 youngsters at a local Boys & Girls Club so they could buy their family members Christmas presents.

"

I'm a Kansas City citizen; I'm around all the time. This is my new home, and hopefully I've made a lot of friends in the city. It's one thing to be a part of an organization. It's another thing to be a part of the community. That's my job here, is to be able to reach out and put smiles on people's faces. That's why I love doing what I do.

"

On helping others and being part of a community, NFL Players Association, 2015.

I've been very fortunate to have a decent head on my shoulders and to be where I am today, but there are people out here who are struggling. For me to take the time to help others is the absolute least I can do.

99

On being appreciative of his position and standing, NFL Players Association, 2015.

The Facts #5

In 2024, Travis made a $100,000 donation through his Eighty-Seven & Running charity to two young sisters wounded in the Kansas City Super Bowl victory parade shooting. The money was donated to the Reyes family as they sought funds for the recovery of their two daughters, who were among more than 20 people injured in a horrific incident that also claimed one life.

Travis is not just an NFL star to our children. He has spent time with them, learning their names, showing them that they matter to him. They just know that he has let them see him as a real person who cares about them. To me, THAT is the biggest gift Travis has given our children and, I think, it sets him apart.

Mary Esselman
The president and CEO of Operation Breakthrough on Travis's impact off the pitch.

"

It's absolutely ridiculous. And to do it on February 1st to throw me into the wolves like that, that was messed up, man. I don't want anything to do with that one, man.

"

Explaining that he wasn't the inventor of the "fade" haircut nor ever claimed to be—though a *New York Times* article indicated as such, ignoring the connection to Black culture and the fact that it had been a popular haircut among Black youngsters for many years, *The Independent*, February 2024.

I feel like it's a duty of mine to make sure that I'm helping out as much as I can, knowing that it's a responsibility.

"

On his resposibility to give back.

"

Man, I'm comedy all the way. I don't know if I'm anything else. I just like to have a fun time and make people laugh.

"

On laughing through life, *New York Post*, February 2024.

Say It Like It Is!

Trav is so good [and] he's obviously the better football player. He's a special person and his personality, the way he carries himself, he's fun to be around, he's smart… and he's just a good-intentioned human being. I wish, in a lot of ways, I was more similar to Trav.

Jason Kelce

Paying tribute to Travis, NBC, October 2023.

"

It's a mindset. He's not worried about the future, he's not regretting the past. He's so present. You can feel that.

"

Rob Riggle

Riggle on Travis's mental strength and sense of the here and now, *Vanity Fair*, June 28, 2023.

Chapter 4

Family, Friends, and Heroes

A bright star both on the grid and off it, Travis's friends and family talk about the full-of-life man behind the player, and he talks about them.

Family, Friends, and Heroes

You stick him into any environment, and he can figure it out. He's just a genuine guy who can get along with anybody. He has enough confidence in himself that he can just hang back and talk to people and not feel out of place.

Zach Collaros

The quarterback in the Canadian Football League and ex-teammate of Travis's discussing Kelce's ability to adapt, *Vanity Fair*, June 28, 2023.

Travis is definitely the best player I've thrown to. With how big he is and the way he is able to run routes and make plays happen is a really rare thing.

Patrick Mahomes

Kansas City Chiefs quarterback praising his teammate Travis, *Vanity Fair*, June 28, 2023.

Travis is definitely my closest teammate. I would say our friendship is more like a brotherhood—we're brothers now and our families get along together. I'm part of his family and he's part of mine.

Patrick Mahomes

On his close relationship with Travis, *Vanity Fair*, June 28, 2023.

Wherever he is, it's the best day ever. Wherever he is, it's the most fun ever. Whatever he's doing is the coolest thing ever.

Rob Riggle

Chiefs fan, golf buddy, and stand-up comedian Rob Riggle on being around Travis, *Vanity Fair*, June 28, 2023.

Travis Kelce is why you coach.
I think of him as one of my sons.
To be able to sit back and see the
success he's having—the Super
Bowl, *Saturday Night Live*—it's
like a proud dad moment.

Butch Jones
Travis' former University of Cincinnati coach and
mentor on his success, *Vanity Fair,* June 28, 2023.

"

Travis has always been Travis. He's been himself the whole time. He's still Travis Kelce. He'll still walk through the stadium and treat everyone like they're his best friend and he's always going to be like that. It hasn't been any different to me.

"

Patrick Mahomes

Teammate and close friend Mahomes on how Travis's increased stardom has not changed him one iota, Pro Football Talk, January 2024.

Family, Friends, and Heroes

I feel like I've been getting asked this question for my entire career: 'What would you feel if you played your brother in the Super Bowl?' The entire time I've been like, 'That's been the goal.' Now that it's actually happening, it's kind of sick. Now someone's gotta send their brother home.

On the realization that he will be up against brother Jason in the Super Bowl LVII, *New Heights*, 2023.

"

F*** you, congratulations.
Go celebrate.

"

Jason Kelce

After suffering defeat to brother Travis in the Super
Bowl LVII, Jason delivers his own special family
congratulations to his kid bro, HuffPost, February
14, 2023.

There were a lot of punches thrown.
It all just stemmed from somebody
being better than the other one, and
the other one not being able to
deal with it.

Donna Kelce

Travis and Jason's mom recalls the brothers'
overly competitive childhood, *People*, 2024.

66

I had finally got to the point where I was looking him eye-to-eye in high school. I picked him up and threw him onto the kitchen floor and knocked the stove off its hinges and everything. We got yelled at by Mom and almost injured Dad in the midst of it all. That's what ended up breaking up the fight—we almost hurt my dad and sent him to the hospital. That was the end of us fighting.

99

Recalling the end of his fights with Jason, *Monday Night Football*, November 2022.

He played a little bit as a true freshman and then my senior year, he was ineligible because he failed a French class. So we missed out on my senior year playing together.

Jason Kelce

Travis's brother explaining how Travis missed the opportunity for them to play on the same team because of failing classes, pagesix.com, September 2023.

66

I love you, you're the only reason
I wear 87. I never told you that, man.
You started the legacy.

99

Revealing the secret of his shirt number after
he was drafted in 2013—87 was the year his brother
Jason was born, *talkSPORT*, January 17, 2024.

If there is a Kelce legacy [of] two brothers making it to the NFL, it all started in 1987 because this big guy was born in 1987.

Paying homage to his brother Jason during a live TV interview, *talkSPORT*, January 17, 2024.

The Facts #6

Jason and Travis Kelce became the first brothers to face off during an NFL Super Bowl in February 2023. Jason's team, the Philadelphia Eagles, were beaten 35–38 by Travis's team, the Kansas City Chiefs.

Family, Friends, and Heroes

The coolest thing about this Super Bowl was that my whole family was there. I got to play against my brother Jason, who is an Eagle, and my mom was on TV more than both of us. My mom, dad and brother are all here tonight.

Recalling the family get-together that was the 2023 Super Bowl, *Us Weekly*, March 6, 2024.

66

You know, people keep asking me what it was like to beat my brother in the Super Bowl. It was pretty awkward especially because after the game we had to ride home together. Our mom drove us there in her minivan. Even though his team lost after being up 10 points at half, my brother is actually really happy for me.

99

On his brother's support after their iconic Super Bowl face-off, *Daily Mirror*, March 5, 2023.

Family, Friends, and Heroes

I'm forever in debt to this guy for putting his name, our name—the Kelce name—on the line. When I say I owe it all to him, I really do.

99

Expressing admiration for big brother Jason and the people he convinced to give him a second chance, *Bussin' With the Boys* podcast, June 2023.

> We were in everybody's household. I'll remember the week of that Super Bowl more than anything that happened during the game.

Reflecting on the 2023 "Kelce Bowl", *Vanity Fair*, June 28, 2023.

Obviously, my brother and I love each other very much. We're cherishing these moments because we know eventually, they'll be gone.

On his relationship witih his brother, *Us Weekly*, March 6, 2024.

"

Travis just has such a zest and virality for life. My daughters, they're so drawn to him immediately—partly because he's gorgeous, but then also he's just a fun human being. He's exciting. He has energy for days. He'll get down on the floor and he'll crawl into a dollhouse. He does whatever they want.

Jason Kelce

On Travis's relationship with his nieces, E! News, September 12, 2023.

The Facts #7

In September 2022, Travis and NFL star (and brother) Jason Kelce launched their podcast New Heights. The title references the Cleveland Heights area where they grew up. The show has proven to be a huge success, reaching No. 2 overall on Apple podcasts.

You know, my brother and I really—a lot of times—we don't talk that much during the season because we get caught up doing our own thing.

Jason Kelce
Revealing the real reason behind launching their podcast *New Heights*.

"

I don't know where it's going, but it's a lot of fun. To be able to just shoot the shit with my brother for a couple hours, those were some of the funniest moments of the season for me. It really just brought us even closer together at this point in our lives.

"

Explaining the "thinking" behind the *New Heights* podcast with Jason, 2023.

66
The fact that I was always doing something with my brother, the fact that I was always doing something with my father, I was never really alone as a kid.

99

On his close relationship with his brother and his dad growing up, The Players' Tribune, December 2, 2020.

Family, Friends, and Heroes

I know he's got my back. I always feel like a little brother when I'm around him, and I always feel like I can learn from him. I wasn't playing sports unless he played them first. I saw him having fun and having success and it just made me want to go out there and do what he was doing.

"

On his relationship with his brother, The Players' Tribune, December 2, 2020.

"
It's wild and kind of surreal.

"

Discussing the prospect of facing brother Jason in the Super Bowl LVII, *New Heights*, 2023.

Family, Friends, and Heroes

I couldn't have a better resource than my brother. He's one of the smartest guys you'll have a conversation with. He knows so much about so many different things.

99

On his relationship with his brother.

66

I've been able to just follow his footsteps through life into the football world. And then, who knows what happens after that?

99

On following in his brother's footsteps,
BANG Showbiz, April 2024.

Chapter 5

The History Boy

Shooting for the stars—Travis isn't one of the NFL's most dyanmic players for no reason. His passion for the game is clear through his numerous accolades…

I always believe that the sky is the limit, and I'm always pushing myself to reach new heights.

99

On constantly striving to be better.

The Facts #8

Travis Kelce became the fastest tight end in NFL history to reach the 800-reception milestone—and did so in just 142 career games played. He is tied with Torry Holt for seventh-fewest games to record 800 receptions by any NFL pass catcher.

When it's all said and done, I think you're going to have very little argument that he's the greatest tight end to play.

Shannon Sharpe

The legendary tight end gives his verdict on Travis.

"

My job is immediately knowing that situation and understanding what my quarterback expects me to do in reaction to it. That's why we practice… and practice… and practice.

"

On practicing to be the best, The Players' Tribune, October 7, 2016.

One of the most bizarre things you can see while playing in the NFL is open field in front of you. It's shocking, honestly. You want to move, but half the time, you give 'em a little Hollywood and then suddenly see all this green in front of you and it's like, 'Oh shit, what happened here?' If you ever are fortunate enough to experience an open field in front of you as a tight end—

and honestly, that's something not many guys at this position ever get to experience in the NFL—the one thing that you know for certain is that there are people faster than you who are right behind you and want you to fumble the ball. **"**

On the rarity of seeing an open field during a game, The Players' Tribune, October 7, 2016.

Not one of y'all said that the Chiefs were gonna take it home this year. Not a single one. Feel that shit? Feel that? And on top of that, next time the Chiefs say something, put some respect on our name.

Telling it like it is to the doubters after the Chiefs recover to win the Super Bowl LVII 38-35 against the Philadelphia Eagles, Larry Brown Sports, February 2023.

"
That accolade, to be the best at
your position in your conference,
you want that on your resume. **"**

On his ability to work with any position.

I really want to be one of the greats. I want to be able to walk somewhere and have people say, 'Oh, that's Travis.'

On what success means to him.

The Facts #9

Kelce has had seven consecutive seasons with at least 1,000 receiving yards, the most of any tight end in NFL history. He also holds the record for most receiving yards by a tight end in a single season, with 1,416 in 2020, and two years later, he reached 10,000 career receiving yards faster than any other tight end.

My passion for this game is never going to change. You're always going to see me have that fieriness to me. That's just the only way I know how to play this game and I love it for that because I get to release that energy and that passion, that anger that I have.

On his passion and releasing his energy during games, *Kansas City Star*, July 27, 2018.

66

When I look in my father's eyes, man, I know that I made him proud. As a son, with a father that loves him and believes in him so much, that's the world. It really is.

99

On making his dad proud being one of the most important successes.

66

Being a tight end doesn't really have much to do with being a great athlete. What's much more important than your athletic ability is your mindset. Because ultimately, your job as a tight end is going to be to perform against somebody who's a better athlete than you in some capacity.

99

On mindset over physicality, The Players' Tribune, October 7, 2016.

66

You have to block linemen who are stronger than you, and fake out defensive backs who are quicker than you. To do that, you almost have to trick yourself into thinking you're better than you are. If your mind isn't right, your body doesn't stand a damn chance.

99

On tricking your mind, The Players' Tribune, October 7, 2016.

When I get the ball in my hands I'm
a different type of athlete.

On the athlete he becomes when he begins to play.

66

As soon as you get complacent with where you are in a game, that's where you come and then it bites you in the rear. So you just want to make sure that you're keeping that energy high, when guys are making plays you're getting excited for them and you're staying locked in through all 60 minutes of the game.

99

On finding energy during a game, *People*, November 4, 2020.

I grew up in the 90s loving the basketball sneakers, and that's where fashion really started for me.

On his love for fashion and style, *Sports Business Journal*, October 27, 2020.

I think the football world is starting to kind of come around to being that fashion-forward mentality. **"**

On football and fashion, *Us Weekly*, December 17, 2023.

The History Boy

My managers and agents love to tell me how underpaid I am. Any time I talk about wanting more money, they're just like, 'Why don't you go to the Chiefs and ask them?'

On not being quite at the pay scale level of some of his contemporaries, bleacherreport.com, June 28, 2023.

66

When I saw Tyreek go and get $30 [million] a year, in the back of my head, I was like, man, that's two to three times what I'm making right now. I'm like, the free market looks like fun until you go somewhere, and you don't win. I love winning. I love the situation I'm in.

99

On the grass not always being greener on the other side, even if the dollar bills are…

The History Boy

You see how much more money you could be making and, yeah, it hits you in the gut a little bit. It makes you think you're being taken advantage of. I don't know if I really pressed the gas if I would get what I'm quote-unquote worth. But I know I enjoy coming to that building every single day.

On refusing monetary gain over job satisfaction— for now!

66

All I can ask for is the opportunity to go out there and beat a man one on one. If you win your one-on-one matchups in this league, you're going to have a lot of success. **99**

On the secret to football success.

The Facts #10

Kelce set the NFL record for most total receptions in playoff games with 165 after his nine-catch performance in the Super Bowl LVIII.

"

Y'all are firing me up, making me want to play right now, baby.
I love the boos more than I love the cheers. Keep 'em coming, Niners Gang, keep 'em coming.

"

Reacting to being booed by 49ers fans at the Super Bowl opening night in Las Vegas—the Chiefs won 25–22, February 2024.

But even when I'm at a clear disadvantage, I always believe I can take the guy across from me. Even when in the back of my head I know there is not a chance in the world, I just try to get after it.

On resilience in the face of defeat, The Players' Tribune, October 7, 2016.

❝

Here's the thing about football (and probably many things in life): nine times out of 10, if you just come off the ball and hit whatever challenge you're facing in the mouth, that's at least a start. Nine times out of 10, you're gonna surprise 'em if you come off the ball and hit 'em in the mouth.

❞

On facing challenges, The Players' Tribune, October 7, 2016.

He was a challenge early. But he's grown up right before our eyes. He's always had that heart, that soft heart, but he had to just grow out of the other stuff, channel it properly.

Andy Reid

The Chiefs coach revealing Travis's maturity both on the pitch and off it, pagesix.com, February 2024.

"

He loves to play the game and he loves to help his team win. It's not a selfish thing. As much as he bumps into me, I get after him. We understand that.

"

Andy Reid

The Chiefs coach laughing off the infamous and very public altercation with Travis during the 2024 Super Bowl, pagesix.com, February 2024.

Hey, come on, you fucker, put
me on.

Letting coach Andy Reid know his feelings on
being sidelined at the 2024 Super Bowl.

> **"**
> As a player, he has always been very good. Now, he had a temper. So on the field, he would go off and do some crazy things. **"**

Andy Reid

The Chiefs coach giving an insight into Travis's temperament during his early years at the Chiefs, pagesix.com, February 2024.

It's definitely unacceptable and I immediately wished I could have taken it back. Coach Reid actually came right up to me after that and didn't even have harsh words for me.

99

Looking back at his infamous Coach Reid outburst with remorse, Sky Sports, February 2024.

"

I can't get that fired up to the point where I'm bumping Coach and it's getting him off balance and stuff. It came in a moment when we weren't playing very well.

"

On remaining calm during games,
Sky Sports, February 2024.

You guys saw that? I'm going to keep it between us unless my mic'd up tells the world. I was just telling him how much I loved him.

Responding to the media's interpretation (via lipreaders) of the 2024 Super Bowl exchange with Coach Reid, *Daily Mirror*, February 15, 2024.

"

Quarterbacks need to keep their emotions in check so that they can always be thinking clearly. But if you want to be a tight end, you need some juice. You're grinding it out in the trenches and catching slants in the no-fly zone. You have to have an edge out there.

"

On using emotions to advantage during a game,
The Players' Tribune, October 7, 2016.

The Facts #11

With 814 catches, Kelce holds the
record for most receptions by an
NFL tight end in his first 10 seasons.
He has caught 19 touchdown passes
in playoff games—a record for the
tight end position. Legendary wide
receiver Jerry Rice, with 22 post-
season touchdown passes, is the
only player at any position to surpass
Kelce's total.

"

To finally throw a touchdown like I used to tell my mom when I was like five years old that I was going to eventually throw a touchdown in the National Football League, I finally got it done. It only took me nine years. That's a good question though, Mom.

"

Answering his mom's question about how he felt after his win when she surprised him at a post-game press conference in Kansas, 2022.

Chapter 6

Talk of the Town

Alongside breaking records on
the grid, Travis continues to conquer
his social and romantic life.

Next stop—the hottest and most
talked-about couple on the planet
have their say...

The Facts #12

Travis became one of the few athletes to host Saturday Night Live on March 4, 2023. The other athletes include Michael Jordan, Charles Barkley, and Peyton Manning.

"

Growing up I was a huge [Chris] Farley, [Will] Farrell, [Jimmy] Fallon kind of guy. I used to watch *Saturday Night Live* with my mother. And it's an absolute honor and privilege to be hosting *SNL* March 4th.

"

Explaining his love for *SNL* on the *Jimmy Fallon Show, Sports Illustrated,* February 16, 2023.

I'll get people yelling at me, 'Hey, SNL was great,' even more than people say, 'Hey, that Super Bowl was awesome'—they were both pretty fun.

On the praise he received when hosting *SNL, Vanity Fair*, June 28, 2023.

"

I think he killed it. He's a natural. He was a presence from the moment he walked out.

"

Lorne Michaels

The legendary creator of *SNL* gives Travis the ultimate thumbs-up, *Vanity Fair*, June 28, 2023.

I wouldn't even say I'm really good at dancing, I'd just say I'm not shy to movement. At a young age, people would laugh at me moving. None of it looked like it should have been called a dance move. But it was just me being goofy. **"**

On his no-so-great dance moves and his love for movement, *GQ*, September 7, 2017.

66
When you see me dancing in the end zone... that's Cleveland Heights.

99

On the inspiration behind his dance moves.

66

I'm dedicated to finding the girl of my dreams.

99

On finding his perfect match.

"

But I wanted to give Taylor Swift one with my number on it. She doesn't meet anybody, or at least she didn't want to meet me, so I took it personal.

"

On his early attempts to woo Taylor Swift—a bracelet with his phone number, *Vanity Fair*, December 6, 2023.

Talk of the Town

When I met her in New York, we had already kind of been talking, so I knew we could have a nice dinner and, like, a conversation, and what goes from there will go from there.

Revealing how he and Taylor Swift began dating, *Wall Street Journal*, December 2023.

> **"**
> I told her, 'I've seen you rock the stage in Arrowhead—you might have to come see me rock the stage at Arrowhead, and we can see which one's a little more lit.' **"**

Revealing an early message to Taylor Swift after she played at the Kansas City Chief's home stadium, *The New Yorker*, September 2023.

I feel like whenever I'm on a date, I'm always having the sense of like, I'm a man in the situation, I'm, like, protective. You always kind of have that feeling—or that self-awareness, I guess.

On his responsibilities in a relationship, Hollywood Life, February 2024.

"

When you say a relationship is public, that means I'm going to see him do what he loves, we're showing up for each other, other people are there, and we don't care. The opposite of that is you have to go to an extreme amount of effort to make sure no one knows that you're seeing someone. And we're just proud of each other.

"

Taylor Swift

The global pop phenomenon on her very public relationship with Travis, *Elle*, February 2024.

I'm happy for my brother that he seems to be in a relationship that he's excited about [and] that he is genuine about. But there's another end of it where it's like, 'Man, this is a lot.' There's some alarms, sometimes, with how over-in-pursuit people can be. Overall, he can deal with some of this.

Jason Kelce

On his little brother's high-profile relationship and the potential pitfalls, *Vanity Fair*, October 25, 2023.

66

I was on top of the world after the Super Bowl and right now I'm even more on top of the world.

99

On his relationship with Taylor, October 2023.

Football is awesome, it turns out.
I've been missing out my
whole life.

Taylor Swift
The superstar finally getting involved in American
football, *Elle*, February 2024.

“
You're all crazy!

”

Responding to suggestions that his relationship
with Taylor Swift is part of a conspiracy to re-elect
Joe Biden ahead of the Super Bowl, *Rolling Stone*,
February 2024.

We're learning with the paparazzi just taking photos from all over the place, but at the same time, it comes with it. You've got a lot of people that care about Taylor, and for good reason. **99**

Watching his profile shoot off the scale because of superstar girlfriend Taylor, *NME*, November 2023.

Taylor, sorry if you're listening Travis. Break up with him. I got a bunch of good-looking single guys that play for the Dallas Mavericks. I gotchu.

Mark Cuban

The Dallas Mavericks owner teasing Travis on ESPN's *First Take* in 2023—Travis responded on X by offering to sign for Dallas on a 10-day contract!

Talk of the Town

Being around her, seeing how smart Taylor is, has been… mind-blowing… I'm learning every day.

On being around Taylor, *Wall Street Journal,* November 2023.

"

Obviously I've never dated anyone with that kind of aura about them… I've never dealt with it. But at the same time, I'm not running away from any of it. The scrutiny she gets, how much she has a magnifying glass on her, every single day… and she's just living, enjoying life. When she acts like that I better not be the one acting all strange.

"

On Taylor's aura and ability to deal with media scrutiny, *Cosmopolitan*, November 2023.

That was the biggest thing to me: make sure I don't say anything that would push Taylor away.

Admitting that friends and family advised him to not say too much in the media about his relationship, November 2023.

66

I'm very aware [of her effect].
Obviously, this is mostly because
Taylor's in my life now. Sure
enough, that brought an entire
entourage of human beings who
just love to support her and love
to support everything that
she's about.

99

On the effect that Taylor has had in his life, *Elle*,
April 2024.

66

Jason Kelce: Trav, you got the number-one bestselling jersey… Followed by me at number two.

Travis: A lot of Swifties over there in the UK. It's gotta be. The only reasonable solution to all of this.

Jason: I'm only number two, because I think that a lot of people in the UK maybe just don't watch football…

and they're like, 'Oh I heard this Kelce guy dates Taylor Swift,' and then they buy my jersey on accident.

"

The brothers discuss the unexpected "Kelce" NFL jersey sales in the UK—ranked as No. 1 and No. 2 bestsellers—and the possible reasons for the merchandise boost… *New Heights* podcast, December 2023.

Talk of the Town

"

I mean, you don't see an entire home team fanbase go insane for somebody wearing the opposite team's colors! Just shows you how amazing that girl is.
They went absolutely insane when they showed Taylor on the screen, yes.

"

Reflecting on Taylor's appearance at a Chiefs game, *New Heights* podcast, December 2023.

"

Shout out to the newest members of the Chiefs Kingdom— Taylor Swift—who has officially reached the Super Bowl in her rookie year.

"

On Taylor Swift, *New Heights* podcast, January 2024.

She's unbelievable. She's re-writing the history books herself, and I told her I'd have to hold up my end of the bargain and come home with some hardware, too.

On aiming to match Taylor's awards with a few of his own, *New Heights* podcast, February 2024.

66

I'm having a blast in life, baby, just flying high. Enjoying it all. Bringing new lives into the football world, opening the football world up to new things.

99

On his experience of being in the spotlight and expanding the football world, *Elle*, April 2024.

Life might not be the party we dream for… But while we're here we might as well dance!

On enjoying life, X, August 2011.

"

I think the values that we stand for and just, you know, who we are as people. We love to shine light on others, shine light around the people that help and support us. And on top of that, I feel like we both have just a love for life.

"

On he and Taylor sharing the same lust for life, *Elle*, April 2024.

It's a beautiful thing, isn't it? And then hopefully, everyone realizes that we're just two people in a relationship supporting each other and having fun with it, man. It's nothing more than that, as much as the world wants to paint the picture and make us the enemy, we just have fun with it.

We enjoy every single bit of it. And sure enough, I love it when Taylor comes to support me and enjoys the game with the fam and friends. It's been nothing than just a wonderful year, man.

99

On the beauty of his relationship with Taylor and the wonderful year he's had, *Elle*, April 2024.

I'm every bit as motivated to get back in and win another Super Bowl. That'll always be my number one job until I retire.

On continuing to achieve Super Bowl wins, *BANG Showbiz*, April 2024.